Easy Tarot:
One Card a Day
for Reflection and Insight

CLARA COOPER

First Published in the U.S. by Copper Canopy Press
Cincinnati, Ohio
Copyright © 2016

All rights reserved. No part of this publication may be reproduced or transmitted in any form or by any means, including informational storage and retrieval systems, without permission in writing from the copyright holder, except for brief quotations in a review.

copper
canopy
press

www.coppercanopypress.com

ISBN 978-0-9967760-1-1

For my spiritual community, Thank You for encouraging me to shine.

Contents

Foreword vi

How to Use This Journal viii

WEEK ONE

Morning Reading   1

Evening Reading   3

Self Reflection   5

Yes or No   7

What Should I Do   9

My Birthday   11

What Do I Need To Know   13

WEEK TWO

Morning Reading   15

Evening Reading   17

Self Reflection   19

Yes or No   21

What Should I Do   23

My Life Theme   25

What Do I Need To Know   27

WEEK THREE

Morning Reading	29
Evening Reading	31
Self Reflection	33
Yes or No	35
What Should I Do	37
My Life Theme	39
What Do I Need To Know	41

WEEK FOUR

Morning Reading	43
Evening Reading	45
Self Reflection	47
Yes or No	49
What Should I Do	51
My Life Theme	53
What Do I Need To Know	55

About the Author — 57

Foreword

Tarot can be intimidating to learn. There are 78 cards that include four suits, numbered cards, court cards, and the Major Arcana. Each card represents a message or a lesson. There are themes that repeat in the deck, but each card has a unique origin and story.

Besides sheer overwhelm, beginners in Tarot sometimes believe there are "bad" cards in the deck like Death, the Hanged Man, and the Fool. Although these cards mean transformation, surrender, and optimism, mainstream culture says that Tarot cards are dangerous and evil. Churchgoers are taught to follow one true God, implying that everything else is not true. Anything that incites questions about the man-made church structure is labeled heretical. If we know ourselves and make our own decisions, the church will lose members. I know this because I threw my cards away fifteen years ago when I joined a church.

At my first introduction to Tarot cards 28 years ago, I saw truth that I'd tucked deep inside. The cards reminded me of what I already knew, but had hidden from the world in order to fit in. Tarot let me set aside my fears, choose my own answers, and claim joy and magic once again. Now that I've left the church, Tarot is my favorite tool for clarity and self-understanding.

In this book, you'll search for your own truth by starting with just one card a day. Doing this gives you more time in reflection, and makes it easy to memorize the feeling and meaning behind each card. You'll quickly learn to read intuitively, without your reference book. Feel free to launch into advanced layouts whenever you wish. If you're already comfortable with the deck, use this journal to further develop your intuition.

Break loose from what binds you, and allow yourself to think of a future of freedom. Listen to your heart, and let your cards find what's been sheltered inside you. Now is your time. Pick up your deck, and believe in yourself.

How to Use this Journal

Prepare your space by clearing a flat surface. Lay out a special cloth, or frame your space with incense, candles, or other items that are special to you. Bring tea or water so you can spend your reading time in comfort.

Place both feet flat on the floor, and sit in a relaxed but upright position. Hold your cards with love, and take three deep belly breaths. Picture yourself in a beautiful outdoor setting. Breathe in the sweet fragrance of your surroundings, and listen to nature around you. Allow yourself to relax in your magical place, knowing you are safe and protected.

Take three more deep breaths, letting your belly relax and expand, and inviting today's chosen question or reflection to come into your awareness. When you are ready, choose a card from your deck. You may fan them out in front of you, or cut the deck and take the top card, or loosely shuffle until one card jumps out.

Once your card is chosen, write its name at the top of the page, and reflect on the message you have for yourself today. Use the lines on the page to explore your truth, and write until the message is complete. When you are finished writing, place your cards back together and hold the deck in your hands. Take three more deep breaths and appreciate your inner wisdom, giving thanks for this special time with yourself.

This journal repeats a seven-day cycle of one-card readings, designed to build your intuition in 28 days.

If you need a Tarot reference book, I recommend <u>The New Tarot Handbook: Master the Meanings of the Cards</u> by Rachel Pollack. My favorite is <u>Tarot Secrets</u> by Amy Lerner and Monte Farber. You can also visit www.learntarot.com for an excellent reference.

Week One

Morning Reading

As you think about your day and all the potential it holds, take a deep breath. Let yourself relax in this quiet moment. Allow your focus to be on the rising sun, and imagine its golden warmth washing over you. Hold the deck in both hands, and let your belly expand out with another deep breath. Close your eyes and breathe. When you are ready, choose a card while asking, "What do I need to keep in mind today?"
Choose your card, and look at it. What does the image tell you? When you feel you've fully explored your own emotional reaction to the card, then look up the meaning in your Tarot reference book. Was your intuition similar to the traditional meaning of the card? How can you take all the information and let it guide you today?

My Card is:

_____
_____
_____
_____
_____
_____
_____
_____
_____
_____
_____
_____
_____
_____
_____
_____
_____
_____

Evening Reading

Get comfortable in your favorite place in your home, and sit in a relaxed, upright position. Hold your cards in your hands and close your eyes to review the events of your day. Think about where you went, who you talked to, and what you carried home with you. See yourself arriving home, and look at the expression on your face. Feel the cards in your hands, and breathe in the comfort of your home. While loosely shuffling the deck, review the events of your day. Let a card jump out, and use your emotions and instinct to see its message. What is your takeaway from today? What lesson should you keep with you?

My Card is:

_____
_____
_____
_____
_____
_____
_____
_____
_____
_____
_____
_____
_____
_____
_____
_____
_____
_____
_____
_____
_____

Self Reflection

Shuffle the cards differently than you have previously. Imagine your face in the mirror, and take a look at yourself. When you're ready, divide the Tarot deck into three piles, and re-stack them randomly. Choose the card that's now on top. Flip it over, and write your impressions of the picture without looking in a reference book. What is the story you see from the image on the card? Write about how that might help you on your current path.

My Card is:

_____
_____
_____
_____
_____
_____
_____
_____
_____
_____
_____
_____
_____
_____
_____
_____
_____
_____
_____
_____
_____
_____
_____
_____
_____

Yes or No

Draw one card, and keep it face down. Think about your question, and imagine the card telling you "yes." What would that mean for your life? Likewise, briefly imagine the answer as no, and what that would mean for you. When you turn the card over, let yourself react emotionally to the image on the card. Feel the answer by simply looking at the image, then write about your gut reaction.

If you aren't satisfied with the answer that you received from your interpretation, try to understand why. Do you hope the situation turns out differently? Use the lines on the page to explore your feelings about this.

My Card Is:

_____
_____
_____
_____
_____
_____
_____
_____
_____
_____
_____
_____
_____
_____
_____
_____
_____
_____
_____
_____

What Should I do?

When there are several approaches you can take, sometimes we need help deciding. Think about the situation, and see each option as a doorway you could enter. Jot some notes around the top of this page or in the margins to represent each choice.

Now that you have some possible outcomes, think about the choice, "no action." What would happen if you disregarded all of those possible options, and held with your current path? Draw a card and let it tell you what would happen if you delayed your decision. Alternatively, you could also draw a card for each of the options you've sketched out.

My Card(s):

_____
_____
_____
_____
_____
_____
_____
_____
_____
_____
_____
_____
_____
_____
_____
_____
_____
_____
_____
_____
_____
_____
_____

My Birth Day

If you are born on the fourth of the month, then use this one card reading on the fourth of this month. Think about the past month and what you've experienced; the people you've met, and how you feel about your life. Draw one card and look at the image. What does this card represent to you for this month, until your next month's birthday? What deep truth are you reminded of? How can this card represent a theme for this month of your life?

My Card Is:

_____
_____
_____
_____
_____
_____
_____
_____
_____
_____
_____
_____
_____
_____
_____
_____
_____
_____
_____
_____
_____

What Do I Need To Know?

When you have an unsettled feeling, there's a message there for you. Again, find a comfortable place where you feel protected. As you let that feeling of uncertainty wash over you, draw today's message of strength from the deck. This card encourages you to take care of yourself first. How will the message of this card embolden you?

My Card Is:

_____
_____
_____
_____
_____
_____
_____
_____
_____
_____
_____
_____
_____
_____
_____
_____
_____
_____
_____
_____
_____
_____

Week Two

Morning Reading

As you think about your day and all the potential it holds, take a deep breath. Let yourself relax in this quiet moment. Allow your focus to be on the rising sun, and imagine its golden warmth washing over you. Hold the deck in both hands, and let your belly expand out with another deep breath. Close your eyes and breathe. When you are ready, choose a card while asking, "What do I need to keep in mind today?"

Choose your card, and look at it. What does the image tell you? When you feel you've fully explored your own emotional reaction to the card, then look up the meaning in your Tarot reference book. Was your intuition similar to the traditional meaning of the card? How can you take all the information and let it guide you today?

My Card is:

_____
_____
_____
_____
_____
_____
_____
_____
_____
_____
_____
_____
_____
_____
_____
_____
_____
_____

Evening Reading

Get comfortable in your favorite place in your home, and sit in a relaxed, upright position. Hold your cards in your hands and close your eyes to review the events of your day. Think about where you went, who you talked to, and what you carried home with you. See yourself arriving home, and look at the expression on your face. Feel the cards in your hands, and breathe in the comfort of your home. While loosely shuffling the deck, review the events of your day. Let a card jump out, and use your emotions and instinct to see its message. What is your takeaway from today? What lesson should you keep with you?

My Card is:

Self Reflection

Shuffle the cards differently than you have previously. Imagine your face in the mirror, and take a look at yourself. When you're ready, divide the Tarot deck into three piles, and re-stack them randomly. Choose the card that's now on top. Flip it over, and write your impressions of the picture without looking in a reference book. What is the story you see from the image on the card? Write about how that might help you on your current path.

My Card is:

_____
_____
_____
_____
_____
_____
_____
_____
_____
_____
_____
_____
_____
_____
_____
_____
_____
_____
_____
_____
_____
_____

Yes or No

Draw one card, and keep it face down. Think about your question, and imagine the card telling you "yes." What would that mean for your life? Likewise, briefly imagine the answer as no, and what that would mean for you. When you turn the card over, let yourself react emotionally to the image on the card. Feel the answer by simply looking at the image, then write about your gut reaction.

If you aren't satisfied with the answer that you received from your interpretation, try to understand why. Do you hope the situation turns out differently? Use the lines on the page to explore your feelings about this.

My Card Is:

_____
_____
_____
_____
_____
_____
_____
_____
_____
_____
_____
_____
_____
_____
_____
_____
_____
_____
_____
_____

What Should I do?

When there are several approaches you can take, sometimes we need help deciding. Think about the situation, and see each option as a doorway you could enter. Jot some notes around the top of this page or in the margins to represent each choice.

Now that you have some possible outcomes, think about the choice, "no action." What would happen if you disregarded all of those possible options, and held with your current path? Draw a card and let it tell you what would happen if you delayed your decision. Alternatively, you could also draw a card for each of the options you've sketched out.

My Card(s):

_____
_____
_____
_____
_____
_____
_____
_____
_____
_____
_____
_____
_____
_____
_____
_____
_____
_____
_____
_____
_____
_____
_____

My Life Theme

In the past week, how has your awareness expanded? Think about what you've experienced since starting frequent reflection with Tarot cards. Have you noticed coincidences or emerging themes in your cards? Draw one card and look at the image. How does this card represent your emerging truth? What themes are making themselves known to you?

My Card Is:

What Do I Need To Know?

When you have an unsettled feeling, there's a message there for you. Again, find a comfortable place where you feel protected. As you let that feeling of uncertainty wash over you, draw today's message of strength from the deck. This card encourages you to take care of yourself first. How will the message of this card embolden you?

My Card Is:

_____
_____
_____
_____
_____
_____
_____
_____
_____
_____
_____
_____
_____
_____
_____
_____
_____
_____
_____
_____
_____
_____
_____
_____

Week Three

Morning Reading

As you think about your day and all the potential it holds, take a deep breath. Let yourself relax in this quiet moment. Allow your focus to be on the rising sun, and imagine its golden warmth washing over you. Hold the deck in both hands, and let your belly expand out with another deep breath. Close your eyes and breathe. When you are ready, choose a card while asking, "What do I need to keep in mind today?"

Choose your card, and look at it. What does the image tell you? When you feel you've fully explored your own emotional reaction to the card, then look up the meaning in your Tarot reference book. Was your intuition similar to the traditional meaning of the card? How can you take all the information and let it guide you today?

My Card is:

_____
_____
_____
_____
_____
_____
_____
_____
_____
_____
_____
_____
_____
_____
_____
_____
_____
_____
_____

Evening Reading

Get comfortable in your favorite place in your home, and sit in a relaxed, upright position. Hold your cards in your hands and close your eyes to review the events of your day. Think about where you went, who you talked to, and what you carried home with you. See yourself arriving home, and look at the expression on your face. Feel the cards in your hands, and breathe in the comfort of your home. While loosely shuffling the deck, review the events of your day. Let a card jump out, and use your emotions and instinct to see its message. What is your takeaway from today? What lesson should you keep with you?

My Card is:

_____
_____
_____
_____
_____
_____
_____
_____
_____
_____
_____
_____
_____
_____
_____
_____
_____
_____
_____
_____

Self Reflection

Shuffle the cards differently than you have previously. Imagine your face in the mirror, and take a look at yourself. When you're ready, divide the Tarot deck into three piles, and re-stack them randomly. Choose the card that's now on top. Flip it over, and write your impressions of the picture without looking in a reference book. What is the story you see from the image on the card? Write about how that might help you on your current path.

My Card is:

_____
_____
_____
_____
_____
_____
_____
_____
_____
_____
_____
_____
_____
_____
_____
_____
_____
_____
_____
_____
_____
_____
_____
_____

Yes or No

Draw one card, and keep it face down. Think about your question, and imagine the card telling you "yes." What would that mean for your life? Likewise, briefly imagine the answer as no, and what that would mean for you. When you turn the card over, let yourself react emotionally to the image on the card. Feel the answer by simply looking at the image, then write about your gut reaction.

If you aren't satisfied with the answer that you received from your interpretation, try to understand why. Do you hope the situation turns out differently? Use the lines on the page to explore your feelings about this.

My Card Is:

_____
_____
_____
_____
_____
_____
_____
_____
_____
_____
_____
_____
_____
_____
_____
_____
_____
_____
_____
_____
_____
_____

What Should I do?

When there are several approaches you can take, sometimes we need help deciding. Think about the situation, and see each option as a doorway you could enter. Jot some notes around the top of this page or in the margins to represent each choice.

Now that you have some possible outcomes, think about the choice, "no action." What would happen if you disregarded all of those possible options, and held with your current path? Draw a card and let it tell you what would happen if you delayed your decision. Alternatively, you could also draw a card for each of the options you've sketched out.

My Card(s):

My Life Theme

In the past week, how has your awareness expanded? Think about what you've experienced since starting frequent reflection with Tarot cards. Have you noticed coincidences or emerging themes in your cards? Draw one card and look at the image. How does this card represent your emerging truth? What themes are making themselves known to you?

My Card Is:

_____
_____
_____
_____
_____
_____
_____
_____
_____
_____
_____
_____
_____
_____
_____
_____
_____
_____
_____
_____
_____
_____
_____

What Do I Need to Know?

When you have an unsettled feeling, there's a message there for you. Again, find a comfortable place where you feel protected. As you let that feeling of uncertainty wash over you, draw today's message of strength from the deck. This card encourages you to take care of yourself first. How will the message of this card embolden you?

My Card Is:

_____
_____
_____
_____
_____
_____
_____
_____
_____
_____
_____
_____
_____
_____
_____
_____
_____
_____
_____
_____
_____
_____
_____
_____
_____

Week Four

Morning Reading

As you think about your day and all the potential it holds, take a deep breath. Let yourself relax in this quiet moment. Allow your focus to be on the rising sun, and imagine its golden warmth washing over you. Hold the deck in both hands, and let your belly expand out with another deep breath. Close your eyes and breathe. When you are ready, choose a card while asking, "What do I need to keep in mind today?"

Choose your card, and look at it. What does the image tell you? When you feel you've fully explored your own emotional reaction to the card, then look up the meaning in your Tarot reference book. Was your intuition similar to the traditional meaning of the card? How can you take all the information and let it guide you today?

My Card is:

_____
_____
_____
_____
_____
_____
_____
_____
_____
_____
_____
_____
_____
_____
_____
_____
_____
_____
_____

Evening Reading

Get comfortable in your favorite place in your home, and sit in a relaxed, upright position. Hold your cards in your hands and close your eyes to review the events of your day. Think about where you went, who you talked to, and what you carried home with you. See yourself arriving home, and look at the expression on your face. Feel the cards in your hands, and breathe in the comfort of your home. While loosely shuffling the deck, review the events of your day. Let a card jump out, and use your emotions and instinct to see its message. What is your takeaway from today? What lesson should you keep with you?

My Card is:

Self Reflection

Shuffle the cards differently than you have previously. Imagine your face in the mirror, and take a look at yourself. When you're ready, divide the Tarot deck into three piles, and re-stack them randomly. Choose the card that's now on top. Flip it over, and write your impressions of the picture without looking in a reference book. What is the story you see from the image on the card? Write about how that might help you on your current path.

My Card is:

_____
_____
_____
_____
_____
_____
_____
_____
_____
_____
_____
_____
_____
_____
_____
_____
_____
_____
_____
_____
_____
_____
_____
_____

Yes or No

Draw one card, and keep it face down. Think about your question, and imagine the card telling you "yes." What would that mean for your life? Likewise, briefly imagine the answer as no, and what that would mean for you. When you turn the card over, let yourself react emotionally to the image on the card. Feel the answer by simply looking at the image, then write about your gut reaction.

If you aren't satisfied with the answer that you received from your interpretation, try to understand why. Do you hope the situation turns out differently? Use the lines on the page to explore your feelings about this.

My Card Is:

_____
_____
_____
_____
_____
_____
_____
_____
_____
_____
_____
_____
_____
_____
_____
_____
_____
_____
_____
_____
_____

What Should I do?

When there are several approaches you can take, sometimes we need help deciding. Think about the situation, and see each option as a doorway you could enter. Jot some notes around the top of this page or in the margins to represent each choice.

Now that you have some possible outcomes, think about the choice, "no action." What would happen if you disregarded all of those possible options, and held with your current path? Draw a card and let it tell you what would happen if you delayed your decision. Alternatively, you could also draw a card for each of the options you've sketched out.

My Card(s):

_____
_____
_____
_____
_____
_____
_____
_____
_____
_____
_____
_____
_____
_____
_____
_____
_____
_____
_____
_____
_____
_____
_____
_____
_____

My Life Theme

In the past week, how has your awareness expanded? Think about what you've experienced since starting frequent reflection with Tarot cards. Have you noticed coincidences or emerging themes in your cards? Draw one card and look at the image. How does this card represent your emerging truth? What themes are making themselves known to you?

My Card Is:

_____
_____
_____
_____
_____
_____
_____
_____
_____
_____
_____
_____
_____
_____
_____
_____
_____
_____
_____
_____
_____
_____

What Do I Need To Know?

When you have an unsettled feeling, there's a message there for you. Again, find a comfortable place where you feel protected. As you let that feeling of uncertainty wash over you, draw today's message of strength from the deck. This card encourages you to take care of yourself first. How will the message of this card embolden you?

My Card Is:

_____
_____
_____
_____
_____
_____
_____
_____
_____
_____
_____
_____
_____
_____
_____
_____
_____
_____
_____
_____
_____
_____
_____
_____

About the Author

Clara Cooper is Clara is on a quest to live in creative flow. In her mid-forties she realized she had wholeheartedly conformed to popular culture, ignoring her own needs. Now back on her path, she uses Tarot cards to help recognize her heart's desires.

She's a graduate of the "Get Your Book Started" coaching program offered through Copper Canopy Press. Clara resides in St. Cloud, Florida.

If you enjoyed this book, please let Clara know! You can reach her online at www.coppercanopypress.com/authors. Your review is also appreciated. Please return to your place of purchase and share your feedback.

www.ingramcontent.com/pod-product-compliance
Lightning Source LLC
Chambersburg PA
CBHW080229020526
44113CB00051B/2633